D0054011

OTHER GIFTBOOKS IN THIS SERIES

happy day   *friend*
hope! dream!   *love*

Printed simultaneously in 2003 by Exley Publications Ltd
in Great Britain and Exley Publications LLC in the USA.

12 11 10 9 8 7 6 5

Illustrations © Joanna Kidney 2003
Copyright © Helen Exley 2003
The moral right of the author has been asserted.

ISBN 1-86187-558-4

Edited by Helen Exley
Pictures by Joanna Kidney

Printed in China

Exley Publications Ltd, 16 Chalk Hill, Watford, Herts WD19 4BG, UK
Exley Publications LLC, 185 Main Street, Spencer MA 01562, USA.
www.helenexleygiftbooks.com

smile

A HELEN EXLEY GIFTBOOK

PICTURES BY
JOANNA KIDNEY

All people smile i

the same language.

PROVERB

SMILES ARE TRIFLES, TO BE SURE;

BUT, SCATTERED ALONG LIFE'S PATHWAY,

THE GOOD THEY DO IS INCONCEIVABLE.

JOSEPH ADDISON (1672–1719)

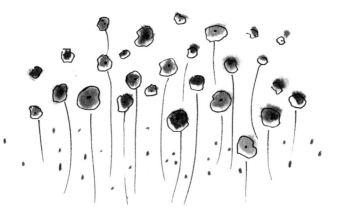

A small smile
from the person at the till,
or the bus driver.
A friendly word from the library assistant.
A cheerful exchange with a man
down a hole in the road.
A civil garage attendant.
And the moment,
the day, is changed.
One's hope in all humanity
is restored!

PAM BROWN, B.1928

A warm smile
is the universal language
of kindness.

WILLIAM ARTHUR WARD

Let there be kindness in your face,
in your eyes and in the warmth
of your greeting.
For children, for the poor,
for all who suffer and are alone,
always have a happy smile.
Give them not only your care,
but your heart.

MOTHER TERESA (1910–1997)

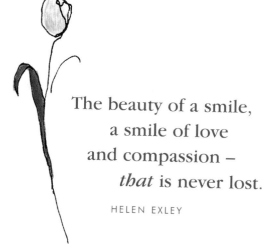

The beauty of a smile,
a smile of love
and compassion –
that is never lost.

HELEN EXLEY

Life is not made up of great sacrifices
and duties, but of little things;
in which smiles and kindness
given habitually are what win and
preserve the heart and secure comfort.

SIR HUMPHRY DAVY (1778–1829)

*Love is rarely to be found
in extravagant gestures.*
*It is mostly revealed in a quiet word
or a gentle smile.*

STUART AND LINDA MACFARLANE

smile (n.) the shortes

stance between two people.

THE WIT'S DICTIONARY [ANON.]

A Child of Happiness
     always seems like an old soul
living in a new body,
     and her face is very serious
until she smiles,
          and then the sun
     lights up the world....

ANNE CAMERON, B.1938

What sunshine
      is to flowers, smiles
are to humanity.

JOSEPH ADDISON (1672–1719)

Humor is a presence
      in the world – like grace –
and shines on everybody....

GARRISON KEILLOR, B.1942

If in our daily life we can smile,
if we can be peaceful and happy,
not only we, but everyone
will profit from it.
This is the most basic kind
of peace work....

THICH NHAT HANH, B.1926

PEACE STARTS WITH A SMILE.

MOTHER TERESA (1910–1997)

The day began with dismal doubt
A stubborn thing to put to rout;
But all my worries flew away
When someone smiled at me today.

AUTHOR UNKNOWN

The first thing to be done
is laughter,
because that sets the trend
for the whole day.

OSHO (1931–1990), FROM "THE ORANGE BOOK"

There are persons so radiant,
so genial, so kind,
so pleasure-bearing,
that you instinctively feel,
in their presence,
that they do you good,
that their coming into a room
is like bringing a lamp there.

HENRY WARD BEECHER (1813–1887)

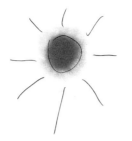

LAUGHTER IS THE JOYOUS,
UNIVERSAL EVERGREEN OF LIFE.

ABRAHAM LINCOLN (1809–1865)

Learn the sweet magic of a cheerful face;
Not always smiling, but at least serene.

OLIVER WENDELL HOLMES (1809–1894)

AN INEXHAUSTIBLE GOOD NATURE IS ONE OF THE MOST PRECIOUS GIFTS OF HEAVEN.

WASHINGTON IRVING (1783–1859)

Cheerful people are like sunshine,
cheering up everybody around them....

HENRY WARD BEECHER (1813–1887)

Actions speak louder than words,
and a smile says,
"I like you. You make me happy.
I am glad to see you."

DALE CARNEGIE (1888-1955)

A SMILE IS THE UNIVERSAL WELCOME.

MAX EASTMAN (1883–1969)

Things are going wrong.
You feel low, a failure...

SMILE! Bare your teeth
if you can't smile from inside.
Fake it if you have to.
Everyone you see will feel better –
and so will you.

JODIE "BUBBLES" ALAN

A good laugh is

sunshine in a house.

WILLIAM MAKEPEACE THACKERAY (1811–1863)

There is no law that lays it down
that you must smile!
But you can make a gift of your smile;
you can be the heaven of kindness
in your family.

KAROL WOJTYLA, B.1920

She is kind and gentle.
Sometimes my mother
really loves me
and she looks at my face
and smiles at me.
I go and sit by her.

BALBINDER KAUR KALSI

For me, human beings'
ability to smile is one of our
most beautiful characteristics.
It is something no animal can do.
Not dogs, nor even whales
or dolphins, each of them
very intelligent beings
with a clear affinity for humans,
can smile as we do.

THE DALAI LAMA, B.1935

Of all the things you wear,
your expression is most important.

AUTHOR UNKNOWN

A smile

is the cheapest

and most effective

rejuvenating

face cream.

HELEN THOMSON

It takes just seventeen muscles to smile
but forty-three to frown.
So do what you've got to do with a smile
and it will take much less effort.

STUART AND LINDA MACFARLANE

Every minute your mouth is turned down
you lose sixty seconds of happiness.

TOM WALSH

The most wasted day of all
is that on which we have not laughed.

SÉBASTIEN CHAMFORT (1741–1794)

No matter how grouchy
you're feeling,
You'll find the smile
more or less healing.
It grows in a wreath
All around the front teeth –
Thus preserving the face
from congealing.

ANTHONY EUWER (1877–1955)

Wrinkles
should merely
indicate where
smiles have been.

MARK TWAIN
(1835–1910)

Smile lines should never
be surgically removed.
The marks of affection
are of more value
than the emptiness
of a false youth.

PAM BROWN, B.1928

Always smile back at little children.

To ignore them

is to destroy their belief

that the world is good.

PAM BROWN, B.1928

Things that make me smile

Walking in the country, after a shower
of snow has fallen makes me smile.
Sighting a robin singing happily to himself,
upon a snowy branch reminds me
of other people's happiness too.
Bright parcels makes me think
of all the people who have thought of me
and bought gifts for me.
Watching a little child undoing a parcel
and seeing his eyes light up
like little stars when he reveals the gift
from its wrapping makes me smile.

CATHERINE POTTER, AGE 14

No one needs a smile quite as much
as he who has none to give.

DEBRA JEPPESEN

LEARN TO GREET YOUR FRIENDS
WITH A SMILE;
THEY CARRY TOO MANY FROWNS
IN THEIR OWN HEARTS
TO BE BOTHERED WITH YOURS.

MARY ALLETTE AYER

When a person is too tired to give you a smile,
give them one of yours.

AUTHOR "LIZ", FROM "THE FRIENDSHIP BOOK
OF FRANCIS GAY 2002"

The best smile of all
is a baby's smile.
It has no guile or calculation.
It is pure joy.

PAM BROWN, B.1928

The baby has learned to smile,
and her smiles burst forth
like holiday sparklers,
lighting our hearts. Joy fills the room.
At what are we smiling?
We don't know, and we don't care.
We are communicating
with one another in happiness,
and the smiles are the outward
display of our delight
and our love.

JOAN LOWERY NIXON, B.1927,
FROM "THE GRANDMOTHER'S BOOK"

It is the small, insignificant,
simple gestures that make life bearable.
A smile, a touch, a word, a kindness,
a concern.

PAM BROWN, B.1928

Some small courtesy may restore
someone's faith in humankind!
Thank god for kindly doctors –
and cheerful ladies at the check-out.

CHARLOTTE GRAY, B.1937

I love smiles and laughter.
If one wants more smiles in one's life,
one must create
the right conditions for it.
...So how does one achieve that?
Certainly not through anger,
jealousy, extreme greed or hatred,
but through loving kindness,
an open mind and sincerity.

THE DALAI LAMA, B.1935

FORTUNE COMES TO THOSE WHO SMILE.

JAPANESE WISDOM

Those who bring sunshine
into the lives of others
cannot keep it from themselves.

SIR JAMES M. BARRIE (1860–1937)

It's the song ye sing,
    and the smiles ye wear,
That's a makin'
    the sun shine everywhere.

JAMES WHITCOMB RILEY (1849–1916)

Is it not a thing divine to have a smile
which, none know how,
has the power to lighten
the weight of that enormous chain
which all the living drag behind them?

VICTOR HUGO (1802–1885),
FROM "THE TOILERS OF THE SEA"

*Laughter can be more satisfying
than honor; more precious than money;
more heart-cleansing than prayer.*

HARRIET ROCHLIN

Every one must have felt that
     a cheerful friend is like a sunny day,
which sheds its brightness
     on all around; and most of us can,
as we choose, make of this world
     either a palace or a prison.

SIR J. LUBBOCK (1834–1913)

The human race has only one
really effective weapon and that is laughter.
Against the assault of laughter
nothing can stand.

MARK TWAIN (1835–1910)

...play a trick on your enemy by smiling.
This may sound absurd, but I assure you
it is true. Just think
of the negativity-world
as an enemy whose strength
can be weakened by your smile.

SRI CHINMOY, FROM "THE WINGS OF JOY"

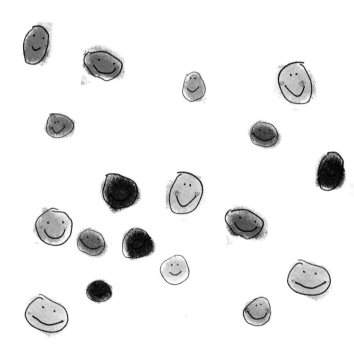

WHEN WE USE THE GIFTS
OF A TEAR AND A SMILE,
THERE IS NO PREJUDICE.

GRANDMOTHER PRINCESS MOON FEATHERS

A traveller walking wearily
into a remote village
and greeted by smiles
finds that village home.

PAM BROWN, B.1928

Smiles are the

language of love.

J.C. AND A.W. HARE

We smile in sympathy, in greeting,
in apology, and in appreciation.
It is without doubt the most important
social bonding signal
in the human gestural repertoire.

DESMOND MORRIS, B.1928

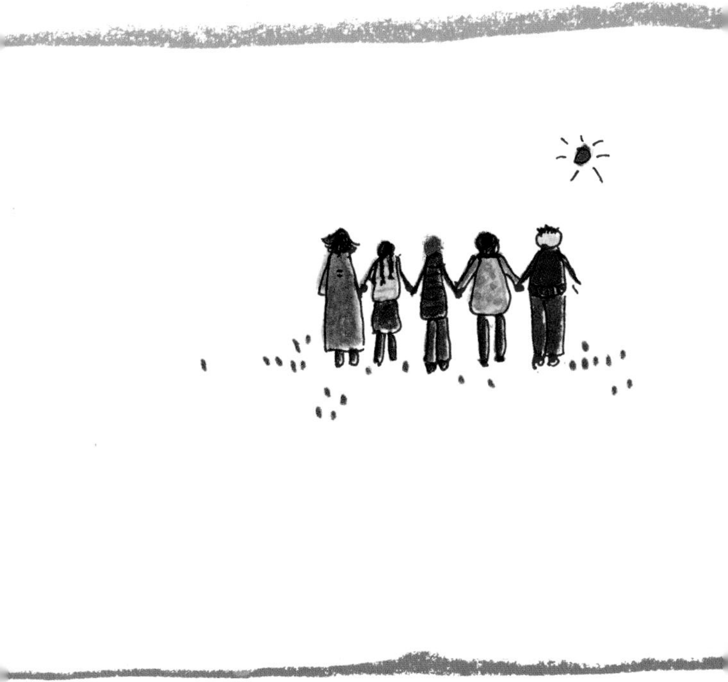

ONE LONELY PERSON.

ONE OTHER

LONELY PERSON.

ONE SHY SMILE,

ONE FRIENDLY GRIN.

TWO HAPPY PEOPLE.

HELEN EXLEY

Friendship, a dear balm...
A smile among dark frowns:
a beloved light:
A solitude, a refuge, a delight.

PERCY BYSSHE SHELLEY (1792–1822)

YOU BRING ME FLOWERS —

BUT YOUR SMILE

OUTLASTS THE FLOWERS.

MAYA V. PATEL, B.1943

One day most of the family
was together in the mailroom,
busily sorting through stacks of letters.
Will was on the floor playing.
He looked up and said, "Mommy,
Daddy can't move his arms anymore."
Dana said, "That's right,
Daddy can't move his arms."
"And Daddy can't run around anymore."
"That's right; he can't run around
anymore." "And Daddy can't talk."
"That's right; he can't talk right now,

but he will be able to."
Then Will paused, screwed up his face
in concentration, and burst out happily,
"But he can still smile."
Everyone put down what they were doing
and just looked at one another.

CHRISTOPHER REEVE, B.1952, FROM "STILL ME"

* * *

For the test of the heart is trouble
And it always comes with the years,
And the smile that is worth
the praises of earth
Is the smile that shines through tears.

ELLA WHEELER WILCOX (1850–1919)

Smiles reach the hard-to-reach places.

STEVE WILSON

Laughing stirs up the blood,
expands the chest, electrifies the nerves,
clears away the cobwebs from the brain,
and gives the whole system
a cleansing rehabilitation.

AUTHOR UNKNOWN

Care to our coffin adds a nail, no doubt,
And every grin so merry draws one out.

JOHN WOLCOT (1738–1819)

Some people
have a beautiful smile
and when people see it they feel happy.

SUSANNAH MORRIS, AGE 10

SALLY HAS A SMILE I WOULD ACCEPT
AS MY LAST VIEW OF EARTH.

WALLACE STEGNER (1909–1993)

May no one

ever come to you

without going away

better and happier.

Everyone should see kindness

in your face,

in your eyes,

in your smile.

MOTHER TERESA (1910–1997),
FROM "HEART OF JOY"

You smiled
and talked to me
of nothing

and I felt for this
I had been waiting long.

RABINDRANATH TAGORE (1861–1941)

Helen Exley runs her own publishing company which sells giftbooks in more than seventy countries. She had always wanted to do a little book on smiles, and has been collecting the quotations for many years, but always felt that the available illustrations just weren't quite right. Then Helen fell in love with Joanna Kidney's happy, bright pictures and knew immediately they had the feel she was looking for. She asked Joanna to work on *smile*, and then to go on to contribute the art for four more books: *friend*, *happy day*, *love* and *hope! dream!*

Joanna Kidney lives in County Wicklow in Ireland. She juggles her time between working on various illustration projects and producing her own art for shows and exhibitions. Her whole range of greeting cards *Joanna's Pearlies* – some of which appear in this book – won the prestigious 2001 Henries oscar for 'best fun or graphic range'.

Acknowledgements: The publishers are grateful for permission to reproduce copyright material. Whilst every reasonable effort has been made to trace copyright holders, the publishers would be pleased to hear from any not here acknowledged. CHRISTOPHER REEVE: Extract from *Still Me* by Christopher Reeve, published by Hutchinson. Used by permission of The Random House Group Limited and Random House Inc. PAM BROWN, HELEN EXLEY, CHARLOTTE GRAY, STUART AND LINDA MACFARLANE, MAYA V. PATEL, HELEN THOMSON: published with permission © Helen Exley 2003.